SELECTED POEMS

by

THOM GUNN

and

TED HUGHES

FABER AND FABER

3 Queen Square

London

First published in this edition 1962
by Faber and Faber Limited
3 Queen Square London W.C.1
Reprinted 1963, 1965, 1967, 1968, 1971 and 1972 (twice)
Printed in Great Britain by
R. MacLehose and Company Limited
The University Press Glasgow
All rights reserved

ISBN 0 571 05019 0

CONTENTS

THOM GUNN

TED HUGHES

THOM GUNN

THE WOUND

The huge wound in my head began to heal
About the beginning of the seventh week.
Its valleys darkened, its villages became still:
For joy I did not move and dared not speak;
Not doctors would cure it, but time, its patient skill.

And constantly my mind returned to Troy.
After I sailed the seas I fought in turn
On both sides, sharing even Helen's joy
Of place, and growing up — to see Troy burn —
As Neoptolemus, that stubborn boy.

I lay and rested as prescription said.
Manoeuvred with the Greeks, or sallied out
Each day with Hector. Finally my bed
Became Achilles' tent, to which the lout
Thersites came reporting numbers dead.

I was myself: subject to no man's breath:
My own commander was my enemy.
And while my belt hung up, sword in the sheath,
Thersites shambled in and breathlessly
Cackled about my friend Patroclus' death.

I called for armour, rose, and did not reel.
But, when I thought, rage at his noble pain
Flew to my head, and turning I could feel
My wound break open wide. Over again
I had to let those storm-lit valleys heal.

THE BEACH HEAD

Now that a letter gives me ground at last
For starting from, I see my enterprise
Is more than application by a blast
Upon a trumpet slung beside a gate,
Security a fraud, and how unwise
Was disembarking on your Welfare State.

What should they see in you but what I see,
These friends you mention whom I do not know?
— You unsuspecting that a refugee
Might want the land complete, write in a tone
Too matter-of-fact, of small affairs below
Some minister's seduction of the Crown.

And even if they could be innocent,
They still applaud you, keep you satisfied
And occupy your time, which I resent.
Their werewolf lust and cunning are afraid
Of night-exposure in the hair, so hide
Distant as possible from my palisade.

I have my ground. A brain-sick enemy
Pacing the beach head he so plotted for
Which now seems trivial to his jealousy
And ignorance of the great important part,
I almost wish I had no narrow shore.
I seek a pathway to the country's heart.

Shall I be John a Gaunt and with my band
Of mad bloods pass in one spectacular dash,
Fighting before and after, through your land,

8

To issue out unharmed the farther side,
With little object other than panache
And showing what great odds may be defied?

That way achievement would at once be history:
Living inside, I would not know, the danger:
Hurry is blind and so does not brave mystery;
I should be led to underrate, by haste,
Your natural beauties: while I, hare-brained stranger,
Would not be much distinguished from the rest.

Or shall I wait and calculate my chances,
Consolidating this my inch-square base,
Picking off rival spies that tread your glances:
Then plan when you have least supplies or clothing
A pincer-move to end in an embrace,
And risk that your mild liking turn to loathing?

TAMER AND HAWK

I thought I was so tough,
But gentled at your hands
Cannot be quick enough
To fly for you and show
That when I go I go
At your commands.

Even in flight above
I am no longer free:
You seeled me with your love,
I am blind to other birds —
The habit of your words
Has hooded me.

As formerly, I wheel
I hover and I twist,
But only want the feel
In my possessive thought,
Of catcher and of caught
Upon your wrist.

You but half-civilize,
Taming me in this way.
Through having only eyes
For you I fear to lose,
I lose to keep, and choose
Tamer as prey.

FOR A BIRTHDAY

I have reached a time when words no longer help:
Instead of guiding me across the moors
Strong landmarks in the uncertain out-of-doors,
Or like dependable friars on the Alp
Saving with wisdom and with brandy kegs,
They are gravel-stones, or tiny dogs which yelp
Biting my trousers, running round my legs.

Description and analysis degrade,
Limit, delay, slipped land from what has been;
And when we groan My Darling what we mean
Looked at more closely would too soon evade
The intellectual habit of our eyes;
And either the experience would fade
Or our approximations would be lies.

The snarling dogs are weight upon my haste,
Tons which I am detaching ounce by ounce.
All my agnostic irony I renounce
So I may climb to regions where I rest
In springs of speech, the dark before of truth:
The sweet moist wafer of your tongue I taste,
And find right meanings in your silent mouth.

INCIDENT ON A JOURNEY

One night I reached a cave: I slept, my head
Full of the air. There came about daybreak
A red-coat soldier to the mouth, who said
'I am not living, in hell's pains I ache,
    But I regret nothing.'

His forehead had a bloody wound whose streaming
The pallid staring face illuminated.
Whether his words were mine or his, in dreaming
I found they were my deepest thoughts translated.
    '*I regret nothing:*

'Turn your closed eyes to see upon these walls
A mural scratched there by an earlier man,
And coloured with the blood of animals:
Showing humanity beyond its span,
    Regretting nothing.

'No plausible nostalgia, no brown shame
I had when treating with my enemies.
And always when a living impulse came
I acted, and my action made me wise.
    And I regretted nothing.

'I as possessor of unnatural strength
Was hunted, one day netted in a brawl;
A minute far beyond a minute's length
Took from me passion, strength, and life, and all.
    But I regretted nothing.

'Their triumph left my body in the dust;
The dust and beer still clotting in my hair
When I rise lonely, will-less. Where I must

I go, and what I must I bear.
   And I regret nothing.

'My lust runs yet and is unsatisfied,
My hate throbs yet but I am feeble-limbed;
If as an animal I could have died
My death had scattered instinct to the wind,
   Regrets as nothing.'

Later I woke. I started to my feet.
The valley light, the mist already going.
I was alive and felt my body sweet,
Uncaked blood in all its channels flowing.
   I would regret nothing.

ON THE MOVE

'Man, you gotta Go.'

The blue jay scuffling in the bushes follows
Some hidden purpose, and the gust of birds
That spurts across the field, the wheeling swallows,
Have nested in the trees and undergrowth.
Seeking their instinct, or their poise, or both,
One moves with an uncertain violence
Under the dust thrown by a baffled sense
Or the dull thunder of approximate words.

On motorcycles, up the road, they come:
Small, black, as flies hanging in heat, the Boys,
Until the distance throws them forth, their hum
Bulges to thunder held by calf and thigh.
In goggles, donned impersonality,
In gleaming jackets trophied with the dust,
They strap in doubt — by hiding it, robust —
And almost hear a meaning in their noise.

Exact conclusion of their hardiness
Has no shape yet, but from known whereabouts
They ride, direction where the tires press.
They scare a flight of birds across the field:
Much that is natural, to the will must yield.
Men manufacture both machine and soul,
And use what they imperfectly control
To dare a future from the taken routes.

It is a part solution, after all.
One is not necessarily discord
On earth; or damned because, half animal,
One lacks direct instinct, because one wakes

Afloat on movement that divides and breaks.
One joins the movement in a valueless world,
Choosing it, till, both hurler and the hurled,
One moves as well, always toward, toward.

A minute holds them, who have come to go:
The self-defined, astride the created will
They burst away; the towns they travel through
Are home for neither bird nor holiness,
For birds and saints complete their purposes.
At worst, one is in motion; and at best,
Reaching no absolute, in which to rest,
One is always nearer by not keeping still.

California

THE UNSETTLED MOTORCYCLIST'S
VISION OF HIS DEATH

Across the open countryside,
Into the walls of rain I ride.
It beats my cheek, drenches my knees,
But I am being what I please.

The firm heath stops, and marsh begins.
Now we're at war: whichever wins
My human will cannot submit
To nature, though brought out of it.
The wheels sink deep; the clear sound blurs:
Still, bent on the handle-bars,
I urge my chosen instrument
Against the mere embodiment.
The front wheel wedges fast between
Two shrubs of glazed insensate green
— Gigantic order in the rim
Of each flat leaf. Black eddies brim
Around my heel which, pressing deep,
Accelerates the waiting sleep.

I used to live in sound, and lacked
Knowledge of still or creeping fact.
But now the stagnant strips my breath,
Leant on my cheek in weight of death.
Though so oppressed I find I may
Through substance move. I pick my way,
Where death and life in one combine,
Through the dark earth that is not mine,
Crowded with fragments, blunt, unformed;
While past my ear where noises swarmed

The marsh plant's white extremities,
Slow without patience, spread at ease
Invulnerable and soft, extend
With a quiet grasping toward their end.

And though the tubers, once I rot,
Reflesh my bones with pallid knot,
Till swelling out my clothes they feign
This dummy is a man again,
It is as servants they insist,
Without volition that they twist;
And habit does not leave them tired,
By men laboriously acquired.
Cell after cell the plants convert
My special richness in the dirt:
All that they get, they get by chance.

And multiply in ignorance.

IN PRAISE OF CITIES

I

Indifferent to the indifference that conceived her,
Grown buxom in disorder now, she accepts
— Like dirt, strangers, or moss upon her churches —
Your tribute to the wharf of circumstance,
Rejected sidestreet, formal monument . . .
And, irresistible, the thoroughfare.

You welcome in her what remains of you;
And what is strange and what is incomplete
Compels a passion without understanding,
For all you cannot be.

II

Only at dawn
You might escape, she sleeps then for an hour:
Watch where she hardly breathes, spread out and cool,
Her pavements desolate in the dim dry air.

III

You stay. Yet she is occupied, apart.
Out of a mist the river turns to see
Whether you follow still. You stay. At evening
Your blood gains pace even as her blood does.

IV

Casual yet urgent in her love making,
She constantly asserts her independence:

Suddenly turning moist pale walls upon you
— Your own designs, peeling and unachieved —
Or her whole darkness hunching in an alley.
And all at once you enter the embrace
Withheld by day while you solicited.
She wanders lewdly, whispering her given name,
Charing Cross Road, or Forty-Second Street:
The longest streets, desire that never ends,
Familiar and inexplicable, wearing
Cosmetic light a fool could penetrate.
She presses you with her hard ornaments,
Arcades, late movie shows, the piled lit windows
Of surplus stores. Here she is loveliest;
Extreme, material, and the work of man.

DURING AN ABSENCE

I used to think that obstacles to love
    Were out of date, the darkened stairs
Leading deprived ones to the mossy tomb
Where she lay carpeted with golden hairs:
    We had no place in such a room,
Belonging to the common ground above.

In sunlight we are free to move, and hold
    Our open assignations, yet
Each love defines its proper obstacles:
Our frowning Montague and Capulet
    Are air, not individuals
And have no faces for their frowns to fold.

Even in sunlight what does freedom mean?
    Romeo's passion rose to fire
From one thin spark within a brace of days.
We for whom time draws out, visas expire,
    Smoulder without a chance to blaze
Upon the unities of a paper scene.

The violence of a picturesque account
    Gives way to details, none the less
Reaching, each one more narrow than the last,
Down to a separate hygienic place
    Where acting love is in the past,
No golden hairs are there, no bleeding count.

No, if there were bright things to fasten on
    There'd be no likeness to the play.
But under a self-generated glare
Any bad end has possibility,
    The means endurance. I declare
I know how hard upon the ground it shone.

THE CORRIDOR

A separate place between the thought and felt
The empty hotel corridor was dark.
But here the keyhole shone, a meaning spark.
What fires were latent in it! So he knelt.

Now, at the corridor's much lighter end,
A pierglass hung upon the wall and showed,
As by an easily deciphered code,
Dark, door, and man, hooped by a single band.

He squinted through the keyhole, and within
Surveyed an act of love that frank as air
He was too ugly for, or could not dare,
Or at a crucial moment thought a sin.

Pleasure was simple thus: he mastered it.
If once he acted as participant
He would be mastered, the inhabitant
Of someone else's world, mere shred to fit.

He moved himself to get a better look
And then it was he noticed in the glass
Two strange eyes in a fascinated face
That watched him like a picture in a book.

The instant drove simplicity away —
The scene was altered, it depended on
His kneeling, when he rose they were clean gone
The couple in the keyhole; this would stay.

For if the watcher of the watcher shown
There in the distant glass, should be watched too,
Who can be master, free of others; who
Can look around and say he is alone?

Moreover, who can know that what he sees
Is not distorted, that he is not seen
Distorted by a pierglass, curved and lean?
Those curious eyes, through him, were linked to these —

These lovers altered in the cornea's bend.
What could he do but leave the keyhole, rise,
Holding those eyes as equal in his eyes,
And go, one hand held out, to meet a friend?

VOX HUMANA

Being without quality
I appear to you at first
as an unkempt smudge, a blur,
an indefinite haze, mere-
ly pricking the eyes, almost
nothing. Yet you perceive me.

I have been always most close
when you had least resistance,
falling asleep, or in bars;
during the unscheduled hours,
though strangely without substance,
I hang, there and ominous.

Aha, sooner or later
you will have to name me, and,
as you name, I shall focus,
I shall become more precise.
O Master (for you command
in naming me, you prefer)!

I was, for Alexander,
the certain victory; I
was hemlock for Socrates;
and, in the dry night, Brutus
waking before Philippi
stopped me, crying out 'Caesar!'

Or if you call me the blur
that in fact I am, you shall
yourself remain blurred, hanging
like smoke indoors. For you bring,
to what you define now, all
there is, ever, of future.

IN SANTA MARIA DEL POPOLO

Waiting for when the sun an hour or less
Conveniently oblique makes visible
The painting on one wall of this recess
By Caravaggio, of the Roman School,
I see how shadow in the painting brims
With a real shadow, drowning all shapes out
But a dim horse's haunch and various limbs,
Until the very subject is in doubt.

But evening gives the act, beneath the horse
And one indifferent groom, I see him sprawl,
Foreshortened from the head, with hidden face,
Where he has fallen, Saul becoming Paul.
O wily painter, limiting the scene
From a cacophony of dusty forms
To the one convulsion, what is it you mean
In that wide gesture of the lifting arms?

No Ananias croons a mystery yet,
Casting the pain out under name of sin.
The painter saw what was, an alternate
Candour and secrecy inside the skin.
He painted, elsewhere, that firm insolent
Young whore in Venus' clothes, those pudgy cheats,
Those sharpers; and was strangled, as things went,
For money, by one such picked off the streets.

I turn, hardly enlightened, from the chapel
To the dim interior of the church instead,
In which there kneel already several people,
Mostly old women: each head closeted

In tiny fists holds comfort as it can.
Their poor arms are too tired for more than this
— For the large gesture of solitary man,
Resisting, by embracing, nothingness.

THE ANNIHILATION OF NOTHING

Nothing remained: Nothing, the wanton name
That nightly I rehearsed till led away
To a dark sleep, or sleep that held one dream.

In this a huge contagious absence lay,
More space than space, over the cloud and slime,
Defined but by the encroachments of its sway.

Stripped to indifference at the turns of time,
Whose end I knew, I woke without desire,
And welcomed zero as a paradigm.

But now it breaks — images burst with fire
Into the quiet sphere where I have bided,
Showing the landscape holding yet entire:

The power that I envisaged, that presided
Ultimate in its abstract devastations,
Is merely change, the atoms it divided

Complete, in ignorance, new combinations.
Only an infinite finitude I see
In those peculiar lovely variations.

It is despair that nothing cannot be
Flares in the mind and leaves a smoky mark
Of dread.
          Look upward. Neither firm nor free,

Purposeless matter hovers in the dark.

INNOCENCE
(to Tony White)

He ran the course and as he ran he grew,
And smelt his fragrance in the field. Already,
Running he knew the most he ever knew,
The egotism of a healthy body.

Ran into manhood, ignorant of the past:
Culture of guilt and guilt's vague heritage,
Self-pity and the soul; what he possessed
Was rich, potential, like the bud's tipped rage.

The Corps developed, it was plain to see,
Courage, endurance, loyalty and skill
To a morale firm as morality,
Hardening him to an instrument, until

The finitude of virtues that were there
Bodied within the swarthy uniform
A compact innocence, child-like and clear,
No doubt could penetrate, no act could harm.

When he stood near the Russian partisan
Being burned alive, he therefore could behold
The ribs wear gently through the darkening skin
And sicken only at the Northern cold,

Could watch the fat burn with a violet flame
And feel disgusted only at the smell,
And judge that all pain finishes the same
As melting quietly by his boots it fell.

THE BYRNIES

The heroes paused upon the plain.
When one of them but swayed, ring mashed on ring:
   Sound of the byrnie's knitted chain,
Vague evocations of the constant Thing.

   They viewed beyond a salty hill
Barbaric forest, mesh of branch and root
   — A huge obstruction growing still,
Darkening the land, in quietness absolute.

   That dark was fearful — lack of presence —
Unless some man could chance upon or win
   Magical signs to stay the essence
Of the broad light that they adventured in.

   Elusive light of light that went
Flashing on water, edging round a mass,
   Inching across fat stems, or spent
Lay thin and shrunk among the bristling grass.

   Creeping from sense to craftier sense,
Acquisitive, and loss their only fear,
   These men had fashioned a defence
Against the nicker's snap, and hostile spear.

   Byrnie on byrnie! as they turned
They saw light trapped between the man-made joints,
   Central in every link it burned,
Reduced and steadied to a thousand points.

   Thus for each blunt-faced ignorant one
The great grey rigid uniform combined
   Safety with virtue of the sun.
Thus concepts linked like chainmail in the mind.

Reminded, by the grinding sound,
Of what they sought, and partly understood,
They paused upon that open ground,
A little group above the foreign wood.

CLAUS VON STAUFFENBERG
of the bomb-plot on Hitler, 1944

What made the place a landscape of despair,
History stunned beneath, the emblems cracked?
Smell of approaching snow hangs on the air;
The frost meanwhile can be the only fact.

They chose the unknown, and the bounded terror,
As a corrective, who corrected live
Surveying without choice the bounding error:
An unsanctioned present must be primitive.

A few still have the vigour to deny
Fear is a natural state; their motives neither
Of doctrinaire, of turncoat, nor of spy.
Lucidity of thought draws them together.

The maimed young Colonel who can calculate
On two remaining fingers and a will,
Takes lessons from the past, to detonate
A bomb that Brutus rendered possible.

Over the maps a moment, face to face:
Across from Hitler, whose grey eyes have filled
A nation with the illogic of their gaze,
The rational man is poised, to break, to build.

And though he fails, honour personified
In a cold time where honour cannot grow,
He stiffens, like a statue, in mid-stride
— Falling toward history, and under snow.

CONSIDERING THE SNAIL

The snail pushes through a green
night, for the grass is heavy
with water and meets over
the bright path he makes, where rain
has darkened the earth's dark. He
moves in a wood of desire,

pale antlers barely stirring
as he hunts. I cannot tell
what power is at work, drenched there
with purpose, knowing nothing.
What is a snail's fury? All
I think is that if later

I parted the blades above
the tunnel and saw the thin
trail of broken white across
litter, I would never have
imagined the slow passion
to that deliberate progress.

'BLACKIE, THE ELECTRIC REMBRANDT'

We watch through the shop-front while
Blackie draws stars — an equal

concentration on his and
the youngster's faces. The hand

is steady and accurate;
but the boy does not see it

for his eyes follow the point
that touches (quick, dark movement!)

a virginal arm beneath
his rolled sleeve: he holds his breath.

... Now that it is finished, he
hands a few bills to Blackie

and leaves with a bandage on
his arm, under which gleam ten

stars, hanging in a blue thick
cluster. Now he is starlike.

MY SAD CAPTAINS

One by one they appear in
the darkness: a few friends, and
a few with historical
names. How late they start to shine!
but before they fade they stand
perfectly embodied, all

the past lapping them like a
cloak of chaos. They were men
who, I thought, lived only to
renew the wasteful force they
spent with each hot convulsion.
They remind me, distant now.

True, they are not at rest yet,
but now that they are indeed
apart, winnowed from failures,
they withdraw to an orbit
and turn with disinterested
hard energy, like the stars.

SONG

O lady, when the tipped cup of the moon blessed you
You became soft fire with a cloud's grace;
The difficult stars swam for eyes in your face;
You stood, and your shadow was my place:
You turned, your shadow turned to ice
     O my lady.

O lady, when the sea caressed you
You were a marble of foam, but dumb.
When will the stone open its tomb?
When will the waves give over their foam?
You will not die, nor come home,
     O my lady.

O lady, when the wind kissed you
You made him music for you were a shaped shell.
I follow the waters and the wind still
Since my heart heard it and all to pieces fell
Which your lovers stole, meaning ill,
     O my lady.

O lady, consider when I shall have lost you
The moon's full hands, scattering waste,
The sea's hands, dark from the world's breast,
The world's decay where the wind's hands have passed,
And my head, worn out with love, at rest
In my hands, and my hands full of dust,
     O my lady.

THE THOUGHT-FOX

I imagine this midnight moment's forest:
Something else is alive
Beside the clock's loneliness
And this blank page where my fingers move.

Through the window I see no star:
Something more near
Though deeper within darkness
Is entering the loneliness:

Cold, delicately as the dark snow,
A fox's nose touches twig, leaf;
Two eyes serve a movement, that now
And again now, and now, and now

Sets neat prints into the snow
Between trees, and warily a lame
Shadow lags by stump and in hollow
Of a body that is bold to come

Across clearings, an eye,
A widening deepening greenness,
Brilliantly, concentratedly,
Coming about its own business

Till, with a sudden sharp hot stink of fox
It enters the dark hole of the head.
The window is starless still; the clock ticks,
The page is printed.

WIND

This house has been far out at sea all night,
The woods crashing through darkness, the booming hills,
Winds stampeding the fields under the window
Floundering black astride and blinding wet

Till day rose; then under an orange sky
The hills had new places, and wind wielded
Blade-light, luminous black and emerald,
Flexing like the lens of a mad eye.

At noon I scaled along the house-side as far as
The coal-house door. I dared once to look up —
Through the brunt wind that dented the balls of my eyes
The tent of the hills drummed and strained its guyrope,

The fields quivering, the skyline a grimace,
At any second to bang and vanish with a flap:
The wind flung a magpie away and a black-
Back gull bent like an iron bar slowly. The house

Rang like some fine green goblet in the note
That any second would shatter it. Now deep
In chairs, in front of the great fire, we grip
Our hearts and cannot entertain book, thought,

Or each other. We watch the fire blazing,
And feel the roots of the house move, but sit on,
Seeing the window tremble to come in,
Hearing the stones cry out under the horizons.

MACAW AND LITTLE MISS

In a cage of wire-ribs
The size of a man's head, the macaw bristles in a staring
Combustion, suffers the stoking devils of his eyes.
In the old lady's parlour, where an aspidistra succumbs
To the musk of faded velvet, he hangs as in clear flames,
   Like a torturer's iron instrument preparing
   With dense slow shudderings of greens, yellows, blues,
     Crimsoning into the barbs:

Or like the smouldering head that hung
In Killdevil's brass kitchen, in irons, who had been
Volcano swearing to vomit the world away in black ash,
And would, one day; or a fugitive aristocrat
From some thunderous mythological hierarchy, caught
   By a little boy with a crust and a bent pin,
   Or snare of horsehair set for a song-thrush,
     And put in a cage to sing.

The old lady who feeds him seeds
Has a grand-daughter. The girl calls him 'Poor Polly', pokes
   fun.
'Jolly Mop.' But lies under every full moon,
The spun glass of her body bared and so gleam-still
Her brimming eyes do not tremble or spill
   The dream where the warrior comes, lightning and iron,
   Smashing and burning and rending towards her loin:
     Deep into her pillow her silence pleads.

All day he stares at his furnace
With eyes red-raw, but when she comes they close.
'Polly. Pretty Poll', she cajoles, and rocks him gently.
She caresses, whispers kisses. The blue lids stay shut.

She strikes the cage in a tantrum and swirls out:
   Instantly beak, wings, talons crash
   The bars in conflagration and frenzy,
     And his shriek shakes the house.

SOLILOQUY OF A MISANTHROPE

Whenever I am got under my gravestone,
Sending my flowers up to stare at the church-tower,
Gritting my teeth in the chill from the church-floor,
I shall praise God heartily, to see gone,

As I look round at old acquaintance there,
Complacency from the smirk of every man,
And every attitude showing its bone,
And every mouth confessing its crude shire;

But I shall thank God thrice heartily
To be lying beside women who grimace
Under the commitments of their flesh,
And not out of spite or vanity.

SIX YOUNG MEN

The celluloid of a photograph holds them well, —
Six young men, familiar to their friends.
Four decades that have faded and ochre-tinged
This photograph have not wrinkled the faces or the hands.
Though their cocked hats are not now fashionable,
Their shoes shine. One imparts an intimate smile,
One chews a grass, one lowers his eyes, bashful,
One is ridiculous with cocky pride —
Six months after this picture they were all dead.

All are trimmed for a Sunday jaunt. I know
That bilberried bank, that thick tree, that black wall,
Which are there yet and not changed. From where these sit
You hear the water of seven streams fall
To the roarer in the bottom, and through all
The leafy valley a rumouring of air go.
Pictured here, their expressions listen yet,
And still that valley has not changed its sound
Though their faces are four decades under the ground.

This one was shot in an attack and lay
Calling in the wire, then this one, his best friend,
Went out to bring him in and was shot too;
And this one, the very moment he was warned
From potting at tin-cans in no-man's-land,
Fell back dead with his rifle-sights shot away.
The rest, nobody knows what they came to,
But come to the worst they must have done, and held it
Closer than their hope; all were killed.

Here see a man's photograph,
The locket of a smile, turned overnight

Into the hospital of his mangled last
Agony and hours; see bundled in it
His mightier-than-a-man dead bulk and weight:
And on this one place which keeps him alive
(In his Sunday best) see fall war's worst
Thinkable flash and rending, onto his smile
Forty years rotting into soil.

That man's not more alive whom you confront
And shake by the hand, see hale, hear speak loud,
Than any of these six celluloid smiles are,
Nor prehistoric or fabulous beast more dead;
No thought so vivid as their smoking blood:
To regard this photograph might well dement,
Such contradictory permanent horrors here
Smile from the single exposure and shoulder out
One's own body from its instant and heat.

THE DOVE-BREEDER

Love struck into his life
Like a hawk into a dovecote.
What a cry went up!
Every gentle pedigree dove
Blindly chattered and beat,
And the mild-mannered dove-breeder
Shrieked at that raider.

He might well wring his hands
And let his tears drop:
He will win no more prizes
With fantails or pouters,
(After all these years
Through third, up through second places
Till they were all world beaters. . . .)

Yet he soon dried his tears

Now he rides the morning mist
With a big-eyed hawk on his fist.

THE JAGUAR

The apes yawn and adore their fleas in the sun.
The parrots shriek as if they were on fire, or strut
Like cheap tarts to attract the stroller with the nut.
Fatigued with indolence, tiger and lion

Lie still as the sun. The boa-constrictor's coil
Is a fossil. Cage after cage seems empty, or
Stinks of sleepers from the breathing straw.
It might be painted on a nursery wall.

But who runs like the rest past these arrives
At a cage where the crowd stands, stares, mesmerized,
As a child at a dream, at a jaguar hurrying enraged
Through prison darkness after the drills of his eyes

On a short fierce fuse. Not in boredom —
The eye satisfied to be blind in fire,
By the bang of blood in the brain deaf the ear —
He spins from the bars, but there's no cage to him

More than to the visionary his cell:
His stride is wildernesses of freedom:
The world rolls under the long thrust of his heel.
Over the cage floor the horizons come.

THE HAG

The old story went that the cajoling hag
Fattened the pretty princess within a fence
Of barbs the spiders poked their eight eyes out in
Even, the points were so close, fattened her
With pastry pies and would not let her incline
One inch toward the threshold from the table
Lest she slip off the hag's dish and exchange
The hag's narrow intestine for the wide world.
And this hag had to lie in a certain way
At night lest the horrible angular black hatred
Poke through her side and surprise the pretty princess
Who was well-deceived by this posture of love.

Now here is an old hag, as I see,
Has got this story direly drastically wrong,
Who has dragged her pretty daughter home from college,
Who has locked up her pretty eyes in a brick house
And has sworn her pretty mouth shall rot like fruit
Before the world shall make a jam of it
To spread on every palate. And so saying,
She must lie perforce at night in a certain way
Lest the heart break through her side and burst the walls
And surprise her daughter with an extravagance
Of tearful love, who finds it easier
To resign her hope of a world wide with love,
And even to rot in the dark, but easier under
Nine bolts of spite than on one leash of love.

ROARERS IN A RING

Snow fell as for Wenceslas.
　　The moor foamed like a white
Running sea. A starved fox
　　Stared at the inn light.

In the red gridded glare of peat,
　　Faces sweating like hams,
Farmers roared their Christmas Eve
　　Out of the low beams.

Good company kept a laugh in the air
　　As if they tossed a ball
To top the skip of a devil that
　　Struck at it with his tail,

Or struck at the man who held it long.
　　They so tossed laughter up
You would have thought that if they did not
　　Laugh, they must weep.

Therefore the ale went round and round.
　　Their mouths flung wide
The cataract of a laugh, lest
　　Silence drink blood.

And their eyes were screwed so tight,
　　While their grand bellies shook —
O their flesh would drop to dust
　　At the first sober look.

The air was new as a razor,
　　The moor looked like the moon,
When they all went roaring homewards
　　An hour before dawn.

Those living images of their deaths
    Better than with skill
Blindly and rowdily balanced
    Gently took their fall

While the world under their footsoles
    Went whirling still
Gay and forever, in the bottomless black
    Silence through which it fell.

THE HORSES

I climbed through woods in the hour-before-dawn dark.
Evil air, a frost-making stillness,

Not a leaf, not a bird, —
A world cast in frost. I came out above the wood

Where my breath left tortuous statues in the iron light.
But the valleys were draining the darkness

Till the moorline — blackening dregs of the brightening
  grey —
Halved the sky ahead. And I saw the horses:

Huge in the dense grey — ten together —
Megalith-still. They breathed, making no move,

With draped manes and tilted hind-hooves,
Making no sound.

I passed: not one snorted or jerked its head.
Grey silent fragments

Of a grey silent world.

I listened in emptiness on the moor-ridge.
The curlew's tear turned its edge on the silence.

Slowly detail leafed from the darkness. Then the sun
Orange, red, red erupted

Silently, and splitting to its core tore and flung cloud,
Shook the gulf open, showed blue,

And the big planets hanging —.
I turned

Stumbling in the fever of a dream, down towards
The dark woods, from the kindling tops,

And came to the horses.
                        There, still they stood,
But now steaming and glistening under the flow of light,

Their draped stone manes, their tilted hind-hooves
Stirring under a thaw while all around them

The frost showed its fires. But still they made no sound.
Not one snorted or stamped,

Their hung heads patient as the horizons,
High over valleys, in the red levelling rays —

In din of the crowded streets, going among the years, the
    faces,
May I still meet my memory in so lonely a place

Between the streams and the red clouds, hearing curlews,
Hearing the horizons endure.

THE MARTYRDOM OF BISHOP FARRAR

Burned by Bloody Mary's men at Caermarthen. 'If I flinch
from the pain of the burning, believe not the doctrine that I
have preached.' (His words on being chained to the stake.)

Bloody Mary's venomous flames can curl;
They can shrivel sinew and char bone
Of foot, ankle, knee, and thigh, and boil
Bowels, and drop his heart a cinder down;
And her soldiers can cry, as they hurl
Logs in the red rush: 'This is her sermon.'

The sullen-jowled watching Welsh townspeople
Hear him crack in the fire's mouth; they see what
Black oozing twist of stuff bubbles the smell
That tars and retches their lungs: no pulpit
Of his ever held their eyes so still,
Never, as now his agony, his wit.

An ignorant means to establish ownership
Of his flock! Thus their shepherd she seized
And knotted him into this blazing shape
In their eyes, as if such could have cauterized
The trust they turned towards him, and branded on
Its stump her claim, to outlaw question.

So it might have been: seeing their exemplar
And teacher burned for his lessons to black bits,
Their silence might have disowned him to her,
And hung up what he had taught with their Welsh hats:
Who sees his blasphemous father struck by fire
From heaven, might well be heard to speak no oaths.

But the fire that struck here, come from Hell even,
Kindled little heavens in his words
As he fed his body to the flame alive.
Words which, before they will be dumbly spared,
Will burn their body and be tongued with fire
Make paltry folly of flesh and this world's air.

When they saw what annuities of hours
And comfortable blood he burned to get
His words a bare honouring in their ears,
The shrewd townsfolk pocketed them hot:
Stamp was not current but they rang and shone
As good gold as any queen's crown.

Gave all he had, and yet the bargain struck
To a merest farthing his whole agony,
His body's cold-kept miserdom of shrieks
He gave uncounted, while out of his eyes,
Out of his mouth, fire like a glory broke,
And smoke burned his sermons into the skies.

OCTOBER DAWN

October is marigold, and yet
A glass half full of wine left out

To the dark heaven all night, by dawn
Has dreamed a premonition

Of ice across its eye as if
The ice-age had begun its heave.

The lawn overtrodden and strewn
From the night before, and the whistling green

Shrubbery are doomed. Ice
Has got its spearhead into place.

First a skin, delicately here
Restraining a ripple from the air;

Soon plate and rivet on pond and brook;
Then tons of chain and massive lock

To hold rivers. Then, sound by sight
Will Mammoth and Sabre-tooth celebrate

Reunion while a fist of cold
Squeezes the fire at the core of the world,

Squeezes the fire at the core of the heart,
And now it is about to start.

MEETING

He smiles in a mirror, shrinking the whole
Sun-swung zodiac of light to a trinket shape
   On the rise of his eye: it is a role

In which he can fling a cape,
And outloom life like Faustus. But once when
   On an empty mountain slope

A black goat clattered and ran
Towards him, and set forefeet firm on a rock
   Above and looked down

A square-pupilled yellow-eyed look,
The black devil head against the blue air,
   What gigantic fingers took

Him up and on a bare
Palm turned him close under an eye
   That was like a living hanging hemisphere

And watched his blood's gleam with a ray
Slow and cold and ferocious as a star
   Till the goat clattered away.

WITCHES

Once was every woman the witch
To ride a weed the ragwort road;
Devil to do whatever she would:
Each rosebud, every old bitch.

Did they bargain their bodies or no?
Proprietary the devil that
Went horsing on their every thought
When they scowled the strong and lucky low.

Dancing in Ireland nightly, gone
To Norway (the ploughboy bridled),
Nightlong under the blackamoor spraddled,
Back beside their spouse by dawn

As if they had dreamed all. Did they dream it?
Oh, our science says they did.
It was all wishfully dreamed in bed.
Small psychology would unseam it.

Bitches still sulk, rosebuds blow,
And we are devilled. And though these weep
Over our harms, who's to know
Where their feet dance while their heads sleep?

CROW HILL

The farms are oozing craters in
Sheer sides under the sodden moors:
When it is not wind it is rain,
Neither of which will stop at doors:
One will damp beds and the other shake
Dreams beneath sleep it cannot break.

Between the weather and the rock
Farmers make a little heat;
Cows that sway a bony back,
Pigs upon delicate feet
Hold off the sky, trample the strength
That shall level these hills at length.

Buttoned from the blowing mist
Walk the ridges of ruined stone.
What humbles these hills has raised
The arrogance of blood and bone,
And thrown the hawk upon the wind,
And lit the fox in the dripping ground.

THRUSHES

Terrifying are the attent sleek thrushes on the lawn,
More coiled steel than living — a poised
Dark deadly eye, those delicate legs
Triggered to stirrings beyond sense — with a start, a bounce,
        a stab
Overtake the instant and drag out some writhing thing.
No indolent procrastinations and no yawning states,
No sighs or head-scratchings. Nothing but bounce and stab
And a ravening second.

Is it their single-mind-sized skulls, or a trained
Body, or genius, or a nestful of brats
Gives their days this bullet and automatic
Purpose? Mozart's brain had it, and the shark's mouth
That hungers down the blood-smell even to a leak of its own
Side and devouring of itself: efficiency which
Strikes too streamlined for any doubt to pluck at it
Or obstruction deflect.

With a man it is otherwise. Heroisms on horseback,
Outstripping his desk-diary at a broad desk,
Carving at a tiny ivory ornament
For years: his act worships itself — while for him,
Though he bends to be blent in the prayer, how loud and
        above what
Furious spaces of fire do the distracting devils
Orgy and hosannah, under what wilderness
Of black silent waters weep.

CLEOPATRA TO THE ASP

The bright mirror I braved: the devil in it
Loved me like my soul, my soul:
Now that I seek myself in a serpent
My smile is fatal.

Nile moves in me; my thighs splay
Into the squalled Mediterranean;
My brain hides in that Abyssinia
Lost armies foundered towards.

Desert and river unwrinkle again.
Seeming to bring them the waters that make drunk
Caesar, Pompey, Antony I drank.
Now let the snake reign.

A half-deity out of Capricorn,
This rigid Augustus mounts
With his sword virginal indeed; and has shorn
Summarily the moon-horned river

From my bed. May the moon
Ruin him with virginity! Drink me, now, whole
With coiled Egypt's past; then from my delta
Swim like a fish toward Rome.

AN OTTER

I

Underwater eyes, an eel's
Oil of water body, neither fish nor beast is the otter:
Four-legged yet water-gifted, to outfish fish;
With webbed feet and long ruddering tail
And a round head like an old tomcat.

Brings the legend of himself
From before wars or burials, in spite of hounds and vermin-
poles;
Does not take root like the badger. Wanders, cries;
Gallops along land he no longer belongs to;
Re-enters the water by melting.

Of neither water nor land. Seeking
Some world lost when first he dived, that he cannot come at
since,
Takes his changed body into the holes of lakes;
As if blind, cleaves the stream's push till he licks
The pebbles of the source; from sea

To sea crosses in three nights
Like a king in hiding. Crying to the old shape of the starlit
land,
Over sunken farms where the bats go round,
Without answer. Till light and birdsong come
Walloping up roads with the milk wagon.

II

The hunt's lost him. Pads on mud,
Among sedges, nostrils a surface bead,

57

The otter remains, hours. The air,
Circling the globe, tainted and necessary,

Mingling tobacco-smoke, hounds and parsley,
Comes carefully to the sunk lungs.
So the self under the eye lies,
Attendant and withdrawn. The otter belongs

In double robbery and concealment —
From water that nourishes and drowns, and from land
That gave him his length and the mouth of the hound.
He keeps fat in the limpid integument

Reflections live on. The heart beats thick,
Big trout muscle out of the dead cold;
Blood is the belly of logic; he will lick
The fishbone bare. And can take stolen hold

On a bitch otter in a field full
Of nervous horses, but linger nowhere.
Yanked above hounds, reverts to nothing at all,
To this long pelt over the back of a chair.

THE RETIRED COLONEL

Who lived at the top end of our street
Was a Mafeking stereotype, ageing.
Came, face pulped scarlet with kept rage,
For air past our gate.
Barked at his dog knout and whipcrack
And cowerings of India: five or six wars
Stiffened in his reddened neck;
Brow bull-down for the stroke.

Wife dead, daughters gone, lived on
Honouring his own caricature.
Shot through the heart with whisky wore
The lurch like ancient courage, would not go down
While posterity's trash stood, held
His habits like a last stand, even
As if he had Victoria rolled
In a Union Jack in that stronghold.

And what if his sort should vanish?
The rabble starlings roar upon
Trafalgar. The man-eating British lion
By a pimply age brought down.
Here's his head mounted, though only in rhymes,
Beside the head of the last English
Wolf (those starved gloomy times!)
And the last sturgeon of Thames.

NOVEMBER

The month of the drowned dog. After long rain the land
Was sodden as the bed of an ancient lake,
Treed with iron and birdless. In the sunk lane
The ditch — a seep silent all summer —

Made brown foam with a big voice: that, and my boots
On the lane's scrubbed stones, in the gulleyed leaves,
Against the hill's hanging silence;
Mist silvering the droplets on the bare thorns

Slower than the change of daylight.
In a let of the ditch a tramp was bundled asleep:
Face tucked down into beard, drawn in
Under its hair like a hedgehog's. I took him for dead,

But his stillness separated from the death
Of the rotting grass and the ground. A wind chilled,
And a fresh comfort tightened through him,
Each hand stuffed deeper into the other sleeve.

His ankles, bound with sacking and hairy band,
Rubbed each other, resettling. The wind hardened;
A puff shook a glittering from the thorns,
And again the rains' dragging grey columns

Smudged the farms. In a moment
The fields were jumping and smoking; the thorns
Quivered, riddled with the glassy verticals.
I stayed on under the welding cold

Watching the tramp's face glisten and the drops on his coat
Flash and darken. I thought what strong trust
Slept in him — as the trickling furrows slept,
And the thorn-roots in their grip on darkness;

And the buried stones, taking the weight of winter;
The hill where the hare crouched with clenched teeth.
Rain plastered the land till it was shining
Like hammered lead, and I ran, and in the rushing wood

Shuttered by a black oak leaned.
The keeper's gibbet had owls and hawks
By the neck, weasels, a gang of cats, crows:
Some, stiff, weightless, twirled like dry bark bits

In the drilling rain. Some still had their shape,
Had their pride with it; hung, chins on chests,
Patient to outwait these worst days that beat
Their crowns bare and dripped from their feet.

RELIC

I found this jawbone at the sea's edge:
There, crabs, dogfish, broken by the breakers or tossed
To flap for half an hour and turn to a crust
Continue the beginning. The deeps are cold:
In that darkness camaraderie does not hold:
Nothing touches but, clutching, devours. And the jaws,
Before they are satisfied or their stretched purpose
Slacken, go down jaws; go gnawn bare. Jaws
Eat and are finished and the jawbone comes to the beach:
This is the sea's achievement; with shells,
Vertebrae, claws, carapaces, skulls.

Time in the sea eats its tail, thrives, casts these
Indigestibles, the spars of purposes
That failed far from the surface. None grow rich
In the sea. This curved jawbone did not laugh
But gripped, gripped and is now a cenotaph.

THE GOOD LIFE

Nothing of profit to be got
So poor-bare to wind and to rain,
His spirit gone to patch his boot,
The hermit returned to the world again.

'Revelation's a burden not to be borne
Save by square-shouldered self-respect.'
But when that latter jaunted bedecked
His vanity was of apparent horn.

'Quiet enough at last I have won,
My body relieved of rag and of ache:
Only a plump, cuffed citizen
Gets enough quiet to hear God speak.'

Loud he prayed then; but late or early
Never a murmur came to his need
Save 'I'd be delighted!' and 'Yours sincerely',
And 'Thank you very much indeed!'

SNOWDROP

Now is the globe shrunk tight
Round the mouse's dulled wintering heart.
Weasel and crow, as if moulded in brass,
Move through an outer darkness
Not in their right minds,
With the other deaths. She, too, pursues her ends,
Brutal as the stars of this month,
Her pale head heavy as metal.